# BUYDOWN SECRETS

## THE UNDERGROUND PLAYBOOK

*For Home Buyers and Sellers Who Are Interested in Saving Thousands of Dollars*

BRAD WARD

**ISBN:978-1-7354035-0-2 (Paperback)**

Published in the United States of America by i How 2 Media

Printed in the United States of America

Cover photography by Rhonda H. Brent

Front and back cover design by Zakaria Nada

Editing by Anne Kirschbaum

**Note**: The information in this book is true and complete to the best of my knowledge. This book is intended only as an informative guide for those wishing to know more about residential real estate financing. In no way is this book intended to replace, countermand, or conflict with the advice given to you by an attorney. This book portrays hopes and dreams for an ideal scenario and the decision to use a buydown should be made by you.

**Disclaimer**: Throughout the book I describe various "hypothetical situations" or anonymous individuals. These descriptions are not of real persons but are either created by me or are amalgams of several different people to illustrate various points in the book. I have altered the facts and descriptions to make it impossible to associate the person described with any specific living individual.

**THIS BOOK WAS GIVEN TO**

**BY**

**ON**

*"Your Big Opportunity May Be Right Where You Are Now."*

**- NAPOLEAN HILL**

*"If somebody offers you an amazing opportunity but you are not sure you can do it, say yes - then learn how to do it later."*

**- Richard Branson**

*"Opportunities multiply as they are seized."*

**- Sun Tzu**

*"Teachers open the doors, but you must enter yourself."*

**- Chinese Proverb**

# INTRODUCTION

When I first spoke with Dan and Nancy, they told me that they had been thinking about buying a home for over a year. Like many first-time homebuyers, they were apprehensive and had anxieties with affordability in South Florida. They had gone online and searched for homes, driven a few neighborhoods and even made an offer on a home which they didn't get because they weren't pre-approved by their bank. Their loan officer at the bank had issued a pre-qualification letter and the real estate agent didn't question the lender about its accuracy. In defense of the real estate agent, she was a good friend of Nancy's, but she had only been licensed to sell real estate for about six months.

We always hear the stories of cash buyers coming in and swooping up homes after their offers are accepted. In reality, the overwhelming majority of residential real estate is financed with a mortgage. If you are a serious buyer, you need to get *pre-approved* because a *pre-qualification* is worth less than the paper it is printed on.

Prior to meeting with Dan and Nancy, I had them fill out an online loan questionnaire to give me a better understanding of their finances and what they would be approved for. After filling out the loan questionnaire, I then had Dan and Nancy send me some documentation which verified their income and allowed me to check their credit. My team and I then packaged Dan and Nancy's loan documentation and sent it to the lender for a full underwriting of their credentials which allowed us to issue a complete pre-approval. With a *pre-approval* in hand, Dan and Nancy resumed their home buying process with the full guarantee that they were approved to purchase a home. In essence, this pre-approval now allowed them to fully compete with all buyers in the market.

If you are a serious buyer, you'll want to make sure that you are pre-approved to make offers with the assurance that you can purchase the property that you are interested in. Not only will this save you time and money, it will also prevent the headaches for the buyer's agent, the listing agent, and the home seller.

I understand that buying a home, especially your first home, is often fun and exciting. And many people fall into the trap of looking for a home prior to working on getting a mortgage. This is like going to the mall without your wallet, or shopping for a car that you cannot afford. It causes unnecessary heartache and disappointment.

Though many people may do some preliminary research on mortgage rates, this does not replace the proper steps of having an underwriter review your credit, your job history, your assets and more importantly, your debt-to-income ratios prior to making an offer on a home.

I did not understand the importance of the pre-approval process when I first got my real estate license in the 1990's. I worked for a broker who told me that the average home buyer looked at 13 homes prior to making an offer and that I should "get the families in the car and show them 13 properties in one day." This sound advice from my broker was great in theory until I wrote three offers and none of the people with whom I had spent time qualified for a mortgage. To this day, I can still feel the pain of learning that the offers were worthless. Not only did I waste my time, I wasted the time of my prospective buyers, the time of listing agents and the time of the sellers. This early failure turned into a blessing and shaped the way I conduct business today. Now, I make sure my clients are fully approved to buy a home before they start looking for homes.

After getting Dan and Nancy pre-approved, I met with them to discuss their financing options. We discussed fixed rate mortgages and adjustable rate mortgages, how long they thought they'd be in the home and how they planned on investing for their futures. These questions and others, and the answers to them can have a profound effect on how families can manage their equity that is advantageous to creating wealth. Everyone's goal should be how they can pay less money to their lender(s) over the shortest period of time.

I also asked them if they'd like to hear how they could reduce their mortgage interest rate by .75%.

And that's what this little book is all about…how you can save thousands of dollars when buying or selling a home.

Dan and Nancy ended up choosing a 7/1 ARM which is a hybrid loan that's fixed for the first 7 years. They chose this loan because they believed they would most likely be in their new home for 5-6 years. The interest rate they received was 3.25% which was .75% less than the prevailing rate of 4% for a 7/1 ARM. That ended up saving them $147 per month, which equates to $1764 per year and $8,820 over five years.

The sellers of the townhome that Dan and Nancy bought estimated that they had saved between $8,000 and $15,000 using a buydown vs. taking a price reduction based on the comparable sales in their townhome community.

Now, as inspiring as buydown can be, I believe the true value of this little-known tactic is how you can use it to change your or someone else's life. Even more rewarding is the impact that this message can have on someone at the right time in their life. That is a real impact. That is powerful.

**THAT is what this book is about.**

Yes-if you use the buydown to your advantage you will save money, and if you are a real estate agent you can use this financing technique to make money. But that's not the point, the buydown is about helping others get what they want.

# Contents

# What I Do

I've been a loan officer and real estate agent (broker) since the 1990's. I really consider myself a Mortgage Planner with the added benefit to my clients of being a Real Estate Broker. I help my clients understand the impact that their mortgages can have in achieving their short-term and long-term financial goals.

My role as a mortgage planner is to empower, educate and show my clients how to build wealth using their mortgage responsibly to their advantage.

## Mortgage Truths:

- A mortgage is never a transaction done in isolation.
- A properly structured mortgage combined with a team of real estate professionals,

CFP's, CPA's, and attorneys can enhance financial planning while creating wealth.

- A mortgage strategy that minimizes interest rate expense while maximizing cash flow should be selected.

- Equity should be managed to increase liquidity, safety and rates of returns from investing.

Mortgage planning is the financial process of carefully evaluating mortgage options and equity maximization for the benefit of the client. A mortgage is most often a family's largest single debt and for most people their home is their single largest investment.

**You should focus on the following questions when selecting a mortgage:**

1. What is your housing, debt planning and cash flow options?

2. What mortgage products and financing tactics would be useful to you?

3. What are the implications for both short-term and long-term mortgage options on your overall wealth building plan?

Mortgage planning is a life-long endeavor because your finances and circumstances change over time.

Anyone who is licensed as a mortgage loan officer can sell you a mortgage. Very few loan officers can help you devise a wealth building strategy and plan for retirement. Every mortgage you get should be used to help you reach your overall wealth building and retirement strategies.

# WHY THIS BOOK

The secret in this book is not restricted to anyone who is buying or selling a home. This technique can be used by real estate agents, loan officers, accountants, financial planners and attorneys to benefit their clients.

Anyone can take advantage of this little-known financing secret to save thousands of dollars.

What if I told you I'm about to share a little-known secret with you that very few people know about?

What if I told you the secrets could absolutely transform the way you buy or sell residential real estate?

What if this technique could be used anytime you buy or sell a home?

What if I told you it doesn't involve budgeting or anything other than simple math?

Are you interested in saving thousands of dollars?

Are you interested in learning more?

This technique is so powerful that I even considered placing a warning on this book's cover stating:

**Warning!!! What you are about to read is contrary to what you think and have been taught about home loan financing.**

*Buydown Secrets* reveals a revolutionary way to think about buying or selling your next home and it can put thousands of dollars into your pocket with extraordinarily little effort.

I've chosen the topic of this book because it's rarely used or even talked about. Most real estate agents, few loan originators and most homebuyers and sellers don't even know it exists.

As you read this little book, I want you to think about and answer this question: "How much will I save using this technique when buying or selling my home?"

If you are a real estate agent, I want you to think about and answer this question: "How much will I save my clients using this technique when they are buying or selling their home?"

In fact, after reading this book (which should take you less than one hour), I'll make you an irresistible offer.

What if I'm so sure that *Buydown Secrets* can save you money that I'll make you a most unusual guarantee?

And here it is: If you don't think that this book is worth at least 100 times what you invested in purchasing it, contact me through social media within 60 days of purchasing this book with your receipt and I'll promptly write you a check for your purchase. No questions asked!

I'm quite sure that this will be the biggest bargain of your life because I'm going to show you what took me years to discover and perfect for my clients.

I'll show you just how I do it for my clients. This financing tactic doesn't require capital, luck, or a bunch of your time.

What does it require?

Belief and mindset. Enough to believe that you can do this and save thousands of dollars for yourself or your clients. Enough belief to learn what I'm going to teach you (I can teach this to a nine-year-old). Enough belief to put the principal into action. When you use a buydown to your advantage, the results will be hard to believe. You'll wonder why nobody taught you this before. Remember - I guarantee it.

You won't have to spend hours learning this concept. I know your time is extremely valuable and that you are busy with your life.

You may soon be saving thousands of dollars or saving thousands of dollars of your client's money. Once again, I guarantee it.

Here's to your success!

# ASSUMPTIONS

I'm going to assume this about you. That you or your clients have a vested interest in residential real estate and residential real estate financing.

I'd further guess that you are most likely selling your home, buying a home, or are a real estate agent, a mortgage loan officer, a CPA, a financial planner or an attorney.

If that's the case, this short little book can save you or your clients thousands of dollars when buying or selling a home.

# STRATEGY VS. TACTICS

There is a difference between strategy and tactics and many people confuse the two. Strategy defines your end result or goal and tactics describes the actions that you take to get there.

For a home seller, the strategy might be to sell their home in the least amount of time and to net the most money after paying closing costs.

The tactics might include having an appraisal done prior to listing the property for sale to get a better sense of the home's value, staging the property for better showings, and making necessary repairs.

On the other hand, a buyer's strategy might be to buy a home in a particular area or school zone and at a great price.

Their tactics might be to buy a home that needs some work or upgrading, making lower than market offers, negotiating seller concessions or designing a maximum budget for their monthly housing expenses.

# MINDSET

What will your mindset be going into the real estate transaction?

For years and through hundreds of mortgage transactions, I genuinely believed that my value was based solely on providing my clients with the lowest interest rate and ensuring that my clients closed on time. In short, I was a transactional mindset broker and didn't consider the ramifications that real estate and real estate financing can have on someone's ability to create wealth.

For most people, getting a mortgage is seen as a one-time event. Borrowers typically "chase a rate" without thinking about the long-term consequences their mortgage can have. Don't get me wrong, most of my clients were extremely happy with my services and referred their friends and family to me. This included my real estate partners.

It wasn't until I started diving deeper into mortgage planning that I realized someone's mortgage is much more than a way to finance their home.

I've been mentored by industry giants Todd Duncan, Stephen Marshall, Tim Braheem, Barry Habib, Dave Savage and Carl White.

Even though I was aware of how discount points worked, I wasn't aware of using them to the benefit of both the seller and buyer in a residential purchase transaction.

**Discounting mortgages is not a new phenomenon, but it is one that isn't usually discussed.**

In fact, I know that most real estate agents and their clients extraordinarily little about it.

It really wasn't until I started learning from Scott Nicholson, Dan Keller and Josh Mettles that I fully understood the power of the buydown strategy.

Discounting a mortgage has been used by new home builders for years as an incentive to get more people into a home. The reason that builders can offer better than market rates is because they have built a buydown into the price of the home.

Stephen Marshall introduced me to the concept of mortgage planning in his book *The Millionaire Mortgage Planner* and said, "put in its simplest form, mortgage planning is about helping clients understand the direct relationships and impact their mortgage has on helping them achieve both their short and long-term financial goals. The vast majority of homeowners failed to connect the dots. They believe their mortgage is no way related to their goals of saving for retirement, savings for college, increasing their net worth, and eventually achieving financial freedom. Nothing could be further from the truth. In reality, for most homeowners their mortgage is the number one item that could most positively affect all these goals."

The most important concepts that I've learned from my mortgage planning practice is that we should view our mortgages and the equity in our homes as a long-term endeavor and incorporate them into our overall retirement and wealth creating strategies.

The number one question that I get from most people buying a home or refinancing their mortgage is "What's your rate?"

This is a fair question, but not the best question they should be asking when shopping for a mortgage.

I frequently shop the interest rates of my competitors and review their advertising disclosures (always in fine print). I do this because the majority of mortgage loan advertising is based on rates. This commodity trap is further conditioned in all of us because we have the ability to scan barcodes with our phones and compare prices online. Real estate and real estate financing are a business built on relationships and local markets and isn't a commodity business.

When people ask me, "What's your rate?" What they really want to know is how they can pay less money to their lender for their mortgage. A buydown fits nicely into this strategy.

In his book *Navigating the Mortgage Maze, The Simple Truth of Financing Your Home,* Dale Vermillion puts it this way, "equity just like stock, is worth nothing until you cash it in. Equity works exactly the same way. It's a dormant asset. Your equity is worth nothing unless you use it. To convert it from a dormant asset to a liquid asset you have to cash it in. This is a principal the majority of people miss."

**I want to reemphasize that your mortgage and your equity have a direct and profound impact on your overall financial planning and retirement goals.**

Your mindset can have a direct impact on how you view equity and whether you see your glass as half-full or half-empty.

Dr. Carolyn Dweck, a professor at Stanford University, in her landmark studies and book entitled *Mindset: The New Psychology of Success,* refers to this as having a fixed mindset versus having a growth mindset. Dweck suggests "that our beliefs are key to happiness and to our misery."

The fixed mindset is all about how individuals stay in the status quo and don't look for opportunities. Whereas a growth mindset looks for opportunities. Is a buydown an opportunity for you?

My value proposition with this book is to teach you just one tactic that can increase your equity and save you money. I chose to focus on buydowns because I believe it is one of the most underutilized tactics that both buyers and sellers can use to their advantage. I also know from experience that the buydown opportunity doesn't come along very often for most home buyers and sellers because people stay in their homes for a long time. But when it does, you need to be prepared to act.

# BE FLEXIBLE

My clients and real estate partners always want to know what made past collaborations successful and how they can do the same thing. I tell them it's always about having an open and honest conversation with all of the parties involved. This includes the buyer, the seller and their real estate agents.

Who I call first is determined on how I enter the transaction.

If it's a buyer I'm working with during the pre-approval process, I'll call their agent first to explain the buydown. Once the buyer finds a property that they are interested in making an offer on, I will call the listing agent to explain how the buydown works and how it can save the home seller money too. I then like to call the seller to explain how the buydown process works and present them with different scenarios comparing a buydown vs. taking a price reduction on their home.

When I'm a partner of the listing agent, I speak with them about how they can more effectively use the buydown to secure more listings and the marketing strategies that can attract more potential buyers to the property. I then reach out to the seller and explain the process to them and discuss the advantages for them to incorporate the buydown in their negotiations with buyers.

**Here are four ideas**:

1. **Simplicity** - Keep it super simple; a buydown is easy to understand and use.
2. **Presenting** - If everyone is open and honest from the beginning, the better the outcome. The more everyone understands each party's goals and timelines the more everyone will succeed.
3. **Action** -Nothing will happen if all you do is think about.
4. **Benefits** - What are the benefits to all the parties involved?

# DEFINE YOUR SUCCESS

A successful transaction means something different to everyone.

To the seller it may mean selling their home for the most money possible in the least amount of time. To a buyer it may mean saving more money on the home that they buy and having a mortgage payment that meets their monthly budget.

For real estate agents it may be getting more buyers or securing more listings.

What is clear is that **YOU** need to define your own success. The only way you can do this is to map it out.

**Here are a few steps to help you with your process:**

1. What does success look like in my real estate transaction? Take a few minutes and write down your end goal.

2. Does a buydown work into my plans? Look at it from a mathematical point of view. The numbers do not lie.

3. How can I get there? It's time to determine the tactics that you'll use to get you there.

4. Who can get me there? In my opinion, this is the most important piece of the puzzle because you need someone who is skilled at negotiating buydowns.

5. Make it happen: Decide that you want to use this tactic and act.

6. Ignore the naysayers: Stop wasting time on what other people think. If you can't ignore them; teach them the buydown math or get them a copy of this book.

# PRE-APPROVAL IS A MUST

You've probably heard that a home buyer should get pre-qualified or pre-approved before shopping for a home. Beware because many people will use the two terms interchangeably, but they are not the same. A pre-qualification is an unverified determination of a borrower's ability to get a mortgage versus a pre-approval which is a verified determination by an underwriter.

I personally won't issue any pre-qualifications because a pre-qualification is based on what a buyer says (this is where the term "buyers are liars" originated) versus a pre-approval where all the borrower's loan documentation, credit, income and assets to close are verified by an underwriter. After the underwriter green lights the file, a "conditional approval" is issued to the borrower subject to the real estate purchase contract, home inspections and the property appraising for the purchase price.

When using the buydown strategy during negotiations, it is imperative that all the parties have an open and honest dialogue about the buyer's qualifications to buy the home. This conversation needs to happen with the assurances that the buyer has the ability to obtain a mortgage and that they can close on the home. There is absolutely no point in beginning the negotiation and offer process without the buyer(s) being pre-approved.

# UNDERSTANDING MARKET VALUE

Market value is the most probable price that a seller should expect in a normal environment. This should be considered a fair sale that is not influenced by job loss, death or bankruptcies.

**Fair market value assumes the following:**

1. Both the buyer and seller are motivated.
2. Both parties are acting in their best interest.
3. Time is given to market the property effectively.
4. The transaction could be closed with cash.

When the buyer obtains financing through a lender, the lender will require an appraisal to protect their interest. The appraiser is the person who locates and analyzes comparable sales in the area and calculates the most likely market value for the sale of the home. Appraisers are required to follow clearly established guidelines and compare the subject property with similar homes that have sold within the past six months. The appraiser will adjust the value based on the differences when evaluating the comparable properties.

## Why Do Appraisals Matter?

Appraisals matter because lenders base the loan amount (mortgage) on the LESSER of the appraised value or sales price of the home. This valuation protects the lender and also ensures that homes aren't overpriced. The local market determines the value of a home and not what the seller thinks the value should be.

Occasionally a seller will try to inflate their sales price to compensate for something that they need…more money. I've seen sellers over inflate their asking price because they need the money for the purchase of their next home and to cover any closing cost that they may be anticipating having to pay.

## What If the Appraisal Comes in Low?

The first thing to look at is the property that the appraiser compared to yours to ensure that the appraiser used home sales that are reflective of the current market conditions in the neighborhood. Appraisers are restricted by geographical area and subdivisions and can't arbitrarily choose homes to use as a comparison. If the appraisal seems in line with the other comparable properties used by the appraiser, the loan amount will need to be based on the lesser of the appraised value or the purchase price. If the appraiser used comparable properties that don't make sense, it's your job along with your agent and loan officer to present more favorable comparable properties to the appraiser for their review.

**Here are three things that can be done if the appraisal comes in at a number not anticipated**:

1. Call the appraiser and give them more favorable comparable(s) and see if they will adjust the appraisal.
2. The buyer may decide to still buy the property at the appraised value.
3. Another appraisal could be ordered.

# UNDERSTANDING HOUSING INVENTORY

Housing inventory measures how many months it will take to sell all the houses listed for sale at the current pace of home sales. For example, if there are 500 homes for sale and 100 homes are selling each month, there would be a five-month supply of homes. If 50 homes are selling each month, there would be a 10-month supply of houses.

A buyer's market occurs when inventory exceeds a six-month supply and a seller's market occurs when there is less than a six-month supply of homes available for purchase.

If the inventory numbers are a lot higher than six months, buyers will have more negotiating power than sellers. In this scenario, home prices will likely move lower, and sellers will most likely accept offers for less than the list price.

A seller's market occurs when inventory is anything less than six months. When inventory significantly falls lower than a six-month supply, home prices are likely to move higher and buyers often will be competing with multiple offers on the home they want.

## Inventory Varies Within Area

Housing inventory can vary by geographic area, subdivision and by zip code. It's important to understand what homes have recently sold for and the inventory availability in your area.

## Days on The Market (DOM)

A home that is newly listed and only on the market for a few days has a better chance to sell at the asking price. When a home has been on the market longer than the area housing inventory supply, it is probably overpriced.

While days on the market may indicate a problem with the home or that it's just overpriced, it may also be an opportunity for the buyer and seller to enter a negotiation. It is true that DOM sometimes identifies an unrealistic home seller, but more often than not it is a great opportunity for the seller and buyer to take advantage of the buydown.

## Listing/Sales Price Ratio

Often the final sales price is not the same as the original listing price. Many real estate professionals track the list-to-sale price ratio of home sales in their local areas.

List-to-sale ratios that fall below 100% generally indicate that most home sellers in the area are willing to reduce their price and negotiate with buyers.

**Warning: the listing price-to-sales ratio can be misleading.**

If you take a look at the profile of *Home Buyers and Sellers Report 2020* put out by the National Association of Realtors every year, you'll see that the report states that the median final sales price throughout the United States was a median of 99% of the final listing price. That's because when a seller lists a house at an inflated price, they will most likely have to reduce their asking price when they don't receive any offers. Sellers often forget that home pricing is determined by the market or what the buyer will pay. As an example, a seller may initially list their home for sale for $400,000 and a month later reduce the asking price from $400,000 down to $375,000. With the house now listed at $375,000. the seller accepts an offer for $365,000 and these numbers determine the "final" list to "sales" price ratio.

# UNDERSTANDING SELLER CONCESSIONS

Whenever someone buys a home, they will have closing costs. These costs can run anywhere from 3-7% of the sales transaction for the buyer.

Seller concessions are closing costs that the seller agrees to pay on behalf of the buyer.

**Closing cost that may be paid by the seller on behalf of the buyer:**

1. **Property Taxes**: Sellers may pay property taxes through the end of the year.

2. **Title Insurance**: Title insurance protects the buyer and the lender from any adversarial claims brought on by someone who claims they have the right to the home's title.

3. **Loan Origination**: These fees cover the price of originating the loan which include processing and underwriting.

4. **Home Inspections**: Inspection fees cover the cost of the home inspection required to get homeowner's insurance and are required by the lender.

5. **Recording Fees**: This fee covers the cost of filing the homebuyer's legal closing documents with their local government.

6. **Appraisal Fee**: This fee covers the cost of an appraisal on the subject property.

7. **Attorney's Fees**: In some states, the buyer is required to have an attorney review their closing documents prior to signing at closing.

8. **Discount Points**: Mortgage points or discount points are an upfront fee paid by the borrower or seller to reduce the interest rate on the borrower's loan.

**Here are the guidelines from Fannie Mae on seller concessions:**

If your down payment is between 10% and 25%, the seller can contribute up to 6%. If your down payment is more than 25%, the seller can contribute up to 9%. If you're buying an investment property, the seller's contribution is limited to 2%, no matter what your down payment is.

If a seller is willing to reduce the listing price further than 3%, then you could do a combination of 3% for the buydown and a percentage for any of the fees above.

It is not uncommon to see price reductions more than 10% of the initial listing price to the final sales price. As I mentioned previously, the listing-to-sale price ratio used by real estate boards and the National Association of Realtors is misleading in my opinion, because I've seen price reductions greater than 10% and yet they use the last listing price in determining their ratios.

## UNDERSTANDING HOW INTEREST RATES ARE DETERMINED

Because most people are shopping mortgages by asking "What's your rate?" I thought I'd explain to you how interest rates are priced by each individual lender.

The money that is available for brokers and lenders to quote interest rates comes from capital markets and is based on the trading of Mortgage Backed Securities (MBS's). The individual pricing by lenders or banks is based on their individual pricing models and individual profitability models for their companies. The money comes from the same capital markets, but the profitability model is determined by each individual lender.

This mortgage interest rate explanation is based on how all lenders price their rates and why they vary from lender to lender. If you're familiar with the game of golf, you'll understand this analogy. When playing golf, each of the 18 holes of a course are scored and rated for someone who is considered a good golfer. Imagine that the $15^{th}$ hole is rated a par five. If you take five strokes to get the ball in the cup, then you would be even for that hole and that would be called par. If you got the ball into the cup with only 4 strokes that would be considered below par. If you scored a six or higher this is known as above par.

Another way to understand this is the old-fashioned number line you were taught in grade school when you learned about positive and negative numbers. Think of a number line with the number zero in the middle. Any number to the left of zero would be a negative number and anything to the right of zero would be a positive number.

The pricing of mortgages works the same way. I'll use an arbitrary interest rate of 6%. This would be the par rate. Any interest rate under 6% would be below par and any rate above 6% would be above par.

Lenders price their loans using a baseline rate; sometimes called the rate of the day. This rate fluctuates on a daily basis and can also fluctuate on an hourly basis depending on fluctuations in the financial markets. Most lenders send out their initial pricing at approximately 10:00 AM EST after reviewing the pricing of mortgage backed securities (MBS) and U.S. Treasury bond pricing. Any intraday pricing can happen when the financial markets dictate it. Lenders are not in the business to lose money and will always increase rates faster than they will decrease them.

Once the baseline is determined, the lender then will add pricing adjustments to the baseline to determine the final rate for the borrower. These adjustments can be for credit scores of the borrower, loan to value, cash out, loan amounts, types of properties, escrow waivers, subordinate financing and length of a lock.

Pricing adjustments are determined by the lender and vary from lender to lender.

For example, assuming a baseline rate of 5%, the borrower could have pricing adjustments of .25% for their credit score and an adjustment for loan to value of .25%. This would be a final rate (if locked) of 5.5%.

Once the final rate is established, it is known as the par rate. The discount rate or above par rate will be calculated on the par rate used in the example of 5.5%.

Buydowns and above par pricing are calculated based on the par rate. If you've heard of a no closing cost loan (there is really no such thing as a no closing cost as there are always closing costs associated with getting a loan) the interest rate is raised to above par financing to finance the closing cost. A buydown is a credit to the borrower and called the discount.

Interest rates are priced in $1/8^{th}$ increments or .125%. For example, an interest rate spread of 4-5% would look like this: 4.0%, 4.125%, 4.25%, 4.375%, 4.5%, 4.625%, 4.75%, 4.875% and 5.0%

# UNDERSTANDING DISCOUNT POINTS

Discount points, sometimes called "mortgage discount points" or "points" are fees paid directly to the lender at closing to buy down the interest rate. Anyone can buy down their rate to get a better interest rate.

A discount point is equal to 1% of the mortgage loan amount on the property.

Here are some examples:

A mortgage of a $100,000 with **one discount point** would require a payment to the lender in the amount of $1,000.

A mortgage of a $300,000 with **one discount point** would require a payment to the lender in the amount of $3,000.

A mortgage of a $300,000 with **two discount points** would require a payment to the lender in the amount of $6,000.

A mortgage of a $700,000 with **two discount points** would require a payment to the lender in the amount of $14,000.

A mortgage of a $300,000 with **three discount points** would require a payment to the lender in the amount of $9,000.

A mortgage of a $500,000 with **three discount points** would require a payment to the lender in the amount of $15,000.

Points or discount points are available to everyone who is obtaining a mortgage for the purchase of a home or refinancing their home.

# UNDERSTANDING A PERMANENT BUYDOWN

A permanent buydown is a little-known mortgage financing technique of negotiating, structuring, and financing a residential real estate transaction. The buydown of the interest rate is permanent until the buyer refinances or sells the home.

This strategy is highly effective because it can save both the home seller and home buyer substantial amounts of money.

The seller pays "discount points" as a seller concession. These are paid at closing which reduces the interest rate for the buyer who is buying the home.

The seller concessions for the discount points are determined prior to loan interest rate being locked and are incorporated in the Contract for Sale/Purchase of the home.

Keep in mind that it is really important that the buyer be pre-approved prior to entering into the negotiation process with the seller and agreeing on the terms, including the buydown into the purchase/sales contract.

# UNDERSTANDING A TEMPOARY BUYDOWN

Though this book discusses the use of a permanent buydown, I feel it's important to understand temporary buydowns and how they differ from permanent buydowns.

A temporary buydown is created when upfront money is placed into escrow with the lender to **temporarily buydown** the interest rate.

This is a subsidy that funds the difference between the temporary buydown rate and the true interest rate. The lender reduces the mortgage payment during the buydown period for the borrower and makes up the difference by taking money from the escrow account and applying it to the monthly mortgage payment.

This temporary buydown will end at a future date in time.

A common temporary buydown is called a "3-2-1." The numbers indicate the buydown interest rate reduction percentage during the first three years of the loan. The interest rate for years one through three is determined by subtracting the percentage from the rate that occurs for years four through thirty.

For example, let's say that the closing interest rate is 7% on a 30-year loan. In this scenario the interest would be reduced to 4% (reduced by 3%) during year one of the loan; in year two the interest rate would be at 5% (reduced by 2%) and in year three the rate would be 6% (reduced by 1%).

In years four through thirty the rate would revert back to the closing rate of 7%.

**AUTHORS NOTE**: This book discusses the use of a permanent buy down where the interest doesn't adjust. It's permanent. With a temporary buydown, the homeowner can be put into the uncomfortable position of feeling "payment shock." For example, with a temporary buydown and using the 7% interest rate above, the homeowner above who has a $400,000 mortgage would go from an initial principle and interest payment of $1,909.66 to a final principle and interest rate payment of $2,661.21 after the temporary buydown period ends. That's a payment difference of $751.55!

# BUYDOWN ADVANTAGES FOR THE HOME BUYER

Most buyers looking to buy a home expect to negotiate unless it is a true seller's market where there are often multiple offers and even price increases.

There are many factors that go into the total cost of someone purchasing a home. The buyer typically considers the desirability of the home for their needs, the offered price, the available cash or savings they have for a down payment, the current mortgage interest rates, closing cost associated with the new loan and other closing cost associated with buying the home.

When a buyer incorporates the buydown tactic into their negotiating strategies, they can accomplish four things:

1. **Permanent Payment Reduction** - The buyer can reduce their interest rate by up to .75% on prevailing interest rates. This can be a significant savings over the life of a loan for the buyer because it continues month after month until the loan is refinanced, or the property is sold.

2. **Buy a More Expensive Home** - The buyer using a buydown can qualify for a larger payment because of the interest rate reduction.

3. **Reduced Monthly Housing Expense** - The buyer using this tactic can reduce their overall monthly housing expense allowing them to keep more of their money versus paying it to the lender.

4. **Faster Principal Reduction** - Because the interest rate is reduced with the buydown, the buyer can increase their equity position in the home faster.

# BUYDOWN ADVANTAGES FOR THE HOME SELLER

Most people selling their homes go through a very emotional period while they are in the process of deciding to sell their home. They often have great memories that they've enjoyed while living in their home and those feelings are often compounded while preparing their home for sale. They must interview listing agents, prepare the home for sale, make necessary repairs, stage it and determine a bottom-line price or net sales price that they are willing to accept.

On occasion, a seller will receive a lowball offer from a buyer and become terribly upset with the offer and stop negotiating. When a seller can detach themselves emotionally from the property, they can often see other opportunities to make the transaction happen. The best negotiations usually occur when there is a benefit for both the buyer and the seller.

When a seller incorporates the buydown tactic into their negotiating strategies, they can accomplish five things:

1. **Marketability** - The home becomes more affordable to a larger segment of the market. This increases the home's marketability because more people can qualify for the mortgage on the property. The National Association of Realtors conducts a yearly survey of recent home buyers and home sellers entitled "Profile of Home Buyers and Sellers." The recent report was mailed out in July of 2019 and was based on a 125-question survey which tracks the trends in residential real estate. The 2020 Profile of Home Buyer's and Seller's revealed that 86% of recent homebuyers financed their home purchases with a mortgage.

2. **Save More Money** -The seller can save money by offering a buydown versus taking price reductions. A 3% contribution to a buyer's mortgage interest rate can reduce the

buyer's interest rate by up to .75% and has more financial power than a 3%+ price reduction.

3. **Gain an Advantage** - The seller can gain a competitive advantage over existing homes listed for sale in their neighborhood because they won't have to take a large price reduction to compete with a lower-priced listing in their area.
4. **Reduce the Risk** - The risk of a contract falling out is reduced because the debt-to-income ratios limits of the buyer are strengthened because of the lower interest rate. They qualify for a larger payment.
5. **Save Even More Money** - The seller can use the same tactic when buying their new home after they learn this negotiating technique. This money saving option can be used when buying second homes and residential investment properties too.

**Buydowns are 300% more effective than a price reduction.**

# 3:1 Ratio

# BUYDOWN SCENARIOS

The numbers couldn't be right… could they? I did the math over and over again and the results were always a 3:1 ratio between a buydown versus taking a price reduction.

The following scenarios are used to show you the real power of using a buydown when buying or selling a home. The interest rate is not important, and neither is the loan amount. I chose a 5% interest rate as an arbitrary number for comparisons and to keep this book evergreen.

What is important is that you understand the 3:1 ratio of a buydown versus a price reduction. There is an undeniable power in this ratio, and it can save you thousands of dollars when it is used.

Unfortunately, too few people know about this or use this powerful tool when negotiating the sale of a home.

To get an accurate picture of your personal circumstances, just replace the 5% interest rate with whatever rate the current market is in.

## Scenarios

### $300,000 Loan Amount

The buyer could get a mortgage in the amount of $300,000 with an interest rate of 5% after negotiating a price reduction on the property and their principle and interest payment would be $1,610.46 per month. Instead, the buyer negotiated a 3% buydown with the seller and the seller is willing to contribute 3% towards the buydown resulting in a loan amount of $300,000 with an interest rate of 4.25% and a principal and interest payment of $1,475. The buyer would need to get a loan for $273,000 at 5% with a principal and interest to get a similar payment of $1,465.52.

### $400,000 Loan Amount

The buyer could get a mortgage in the amount of $400,000 with an interest rate of 5% after negotiating a price reduction on the property and their principle and interest payment would be $2,147.29 per month. Instead, the buyer negotiated a 3% buydown with the seller and the seller is willing to contribute 3% towards the buydown resulting in a loan amount of $400,000 with an interest rate of 4.25% and a principal and interest payment of $1,967.76. The buyer would need to get a loan for $364,000 at 5% with a principal and interest to get a similar payment of $1954.04.

**$500,000 Loan Amount**

The buyer could get a mortgage in the amount of $500,000 with an interest rate of 5% after negotiating a price reduction on the property and their principle and interest payment would be $2,684.11 per month. Instead, the buyer negotiated a 3% buydown with the seller and the seller is willing to contribute 3% towards the buydown resulting in a loan amount of $500,000 with an interest rate of 4.25% and a principle and interest payment of $2,459.70. The buyer would need to get a loan for $455,000 at 5% with a principal and interest to get a similar payment of $2442.54.

**$700,000 Loan Amount**

The buyer could get a mortgage in the amount of $700,000 with an interest rate of 5% after negotiating a price reduction on the property and their principle and interest payment would be $3,757.75 per month. Instead, the buyer negotiated a 3% buydown with the seller and the seller is willing to contribute 3% towards the buydown resulting in a loan amount of $700,000 with an interest rate of 4.25% and a principal and interest payment of $3,443.58. The buyer would need to get a loan for $637,000 at 5% with a principal and interest to get a similar payment of $3,419.55.

**$700,000 Loan Amount**

The buyer could get a mortgage in the amount of $700,000 with an interest rate of 5% after negotiating a price reduction on the property and their principle and interest payment would be $3,757.75 per month. Instead, the buyer negotiated a 3% buydown with the seller and the seller is willing to contribute 3% towards the buydown resulting in a loan amount of $700,000 with an interest rate of 4.25% and a principal and interest payment of $3,443.58. The buyer would need to get a loan for $637,000 at 5% with a principal and interest to get a similar payment of $3,419.55.

**$900,000 Loan Amount**

The buyer could get a mortgage in the amount of $900,000 with an interest rate of 5% after negotiating a price reduction on the property and their principle and interest payment would be $4,831.39 per month. Instead, the buyer negotiated a 3% buy down with the seller and the seller is willing to contribute 3% towards the buy down resulting in a loan amount of $700,000 with an interest rate of 4.25% and a principal and interest payment of $4,427.46. The buyer would need to get a loan for $819,000 at 5% with a principal and interest to get a similar payment of $4,396.51.

**$1,100,000 Loan Amount**

The buyer could get a mortgage in the amount of $1,100,000 with an interest rate of 5% after negotiating a price reduction on the property and their principle and interest payment would be $5,905.04 per month. Instead, the buyer negotiated a 3% buydown with the seller and the seller is willing to contribute 3% towards the buydown resulting in a loan amount of $1,100,000 with an interest rate of 4.25% and a principal and interest payment of $5,411.34. The buyer would need to get a loan for

$1,001,000 at 5% with a principal and interest to get a similar payment of $5,373.58.

**$1,500,000 Loan Amount**

The buyer could get a mortgage in the amount of $1,500,000 with an interest rate of 5% after negotiating a price reduction on the property and their principle and interest payment would be $8,052.32 per month. Instead, the buyer negotiated a 3% buydown with the seller and the seller is willing to contribute 3% towards the buydown resulting in a loan amount of $1,500,000 with an interest rate of 4.25% and a principal and interest payment of $7,379.10. The buyer would need to get a loan for $1,411,000 at 5% with a principal and interest to get a similar payment of $7576.43.

**Authors Note:** Some of the examples used above exceed the Fannie Mae and Freddie Mac loan limit amounts. These "jumbo loans" still allow for seller concessions and buydowns that are determined by each individual lender and their respective lending guidelines.

# PUTTING PEN PAPER TO PAPER

Everybody comprehends things that they can see and read. My suggestion is that you make it tangible and work the numbers out on paper before presenting any offers.

If you are the home seller, you should workout the numbers knowing your bottom line or the net proceeds you are willing to take from the sale of property.

I personally use loan analysis software to make side-by side mortgage analysis for my clients. These comparisons make a real difference when entering into the negotiation process.

I provide a loan analysis for both the buyer and seller that clearly explains everything in a clear and concise fashion and shows the advantages of the buydown for both parties.

You can also do this by hand by putting pen to paper. It is really simple math. Remember that each point or discount point equates to 1% of the loan amount.

Do the math for both parties. If you are the home seller complete the math for the buyer and if you are a buyer do the math for the seller. You can get your real estate agent to help you with this too, though I suggest strongly that this process should be done by a loan advisor who will have better access to lenders and their interest rate pricing.

If you are a seller, workout your savings on the next property you will be buying as well.

Remember this technique can be used over and over again to save you thousands and thousands of dollars.

Writing it down or using software is a great way to gain perspective for making decisions that can benefit both the buyer and seller.

# BEFORE NEGOTIATING

A clear understanding of your buydown objective is paramount. And the time to decide whether a buydown is advantageous to you is prior to presenting or accepting an offer on the home.

Please do not attempt to incorporate the use of a buydown after a contract for sale has been finalized. I've had a few clients call me looking to take advantage of the buydown after the contract has been finalized by both parties and this doesn't work.

Plan ahead and communicate with everyone involved in the transaction. Your communication will be extremely helpful, and they'll appreciate you for your communication.

## Negotiating Tips:

1. **Know Your Market**: As I mentioned before, you need to understand your local market. Markets can fluctuate by price range and subdivision.

2. **Know Your Local Housing Inventory**: Inventory affects the pricing of homes.

3. **Know Days on Market (DOM)**: The more days on the market can affect the buyer and seller's attitudes when entering into a negotiation.

4. **Be Honest and Open**: You can negotiate without giving away your position or bottom line pricing in the transaction.

# MEETING IN PERSON

Before you decide to use a buydown as a tactic to save money, try your best to meet in person.

As I write this in 2020, COVID-19 is spreading around the world and I am in lockdown in Florida. Though we can't meet in person, I have become proficient in conducting video conference calls. We have seen our children go to school virtually and witnessed people on TV who have been conducting interviews virtually online. This may be the new normal.

Don't get me wrong, I still believe that it is best to meet knee to knee with people. In doing this, you get to read each other's body language and have a better chance to create friendships, but it's not necessary. I can present and show my presentation to all the parties online via video.

## Here are some meeting suggestions:

1. **Be Optimistic** - Assume you will be creating a win-win for all the parties involved.

2. **Know the Numbers** - If one party doesn't know their numbers or the other party's numbers, your chances of success become minimized.

3. **Be Open** - Let everyone know what's going on. Discuss objectives, financing, timelines and be flexible.

4. **Be Nice** - I'm amazed with some people's attitudes. Make sure you thank everyone for joining the meeting. Ask them how they are doing? Tell them why you want to do this. Don't be adversarial. Treat people like you want to be treated. Ask yourself, what you would do if the roles were reversed? You want everyone to be on your side. This is a team effort.

# DEAL KILLERS

Do you know what one of the biggest deal killers in real estate is?

If you guessed an agent, you'd be on the right track. Unfortunately, I've seen firsthand too many transactions "crap out" during the negotiation process because of an agent. Sadly, this needless jockeying for control only hurts the buyer and seller.

Many agents feel because they have a real estate license that they are negotiating on their own properties. I've personally had agents tell me "my buyer or seller wouldn't go for that."

This is one of the reasons I chose to write this book, to educate both real estate agents and their prospective real estate clients on the real power of using buydowns.

Not everyone will choose to incorporate a buydown into their real estate plans, but that is not the point.

My point is that everyone should understand all of their options when deciding to buy or sell residential real estate.

A great agent will present all opportunities, solutions and offers to their clients, allowing the client to make an informed decision that benefits them.

# CONCLUSION

## Dear Reader,

I know this book has been easy to read. That's the beauty of this little known "secret." Unlike most mortgage books that focus on the complexities of a mortgage transaction, I wanted to give you an extremely specific tactic to maximize your equity. My goal wasn't to just give you a fish, my goal was to teach you to fish and make more money doing it.

Now that you've finished the book, you're probably asking yourself "What should I do next?" This book is meant to be used as a multi-thousand-dollar playbook. Imagine how much money it can save when buying or selling your next home. This powerful tactic can be used over and over again.

For right now, though, I encourage you to think of all the people including yourself who will benefit from this book. I recommend you do this while the buydown is fresh in your mind:

1. **Who will this help**: Decide who you know who this book could really help? Who do you know who's buying or selling a home? Teach them the Buydown Secret or give them a copy of this book.

2. **Home Buyers**: How much money will you save using a buydown? Write it down.

3. **Home Sellers**: How much money will you save when selling your home? Don't forget to figure out how much money you will save when buying your next home too? Write it down.

4. **Listing Agents**: How much money can you save your clients and how can you effectively incorporate this tactic into your listing presentations? How will you use a buydown to market and attract more buyers? Write it down.

5. **Buyer Agents**: How can you use this tactic to benefit your buyers? Write it down.

This little-known tactic is proven to work. Use it to your advantage to save thousands of dollars in equity and create equity faster. I hope you can see the benefits of using this simple tactic for yourself or your clients. This secret can be used to find more of your dream clients and serve them in a way that really matters to them.

Thank you for allowing me to serve you through this little book. I'm grateful for your time, and I can't wait to see what you do with the buydown secrets that you've learned. Please reach out to me on social media and say hello or if you have any questions.

To your buydown success,

Brad Ward

P.S. This book is available at wholesale pricing to give to your friends and clients. Please contact me for more information about pricing.

Made in the USA
Monee, IL
04 November 2026

67387539R00046